This journal belongs to

....

Date

....

The Confident WOMAN journal

JOYCE MEYER

Ellie Claire
Hachette Book Group
1290 Avenue of the Americas, New York, NY 10104
ellieclaire.com

First Edition: LeatherLuxe® (March 2021)

Ellie Claire is a division of Hachette Book Group, Inc.
The Ellie Claire name and logo are trademarks of Hachette Book Group, Inc.

The publisher is not responsible for websites (or their content) that are not owned by the publisher.

Unless otherwise noted, the quotes in this book were taken from Joyce Meyer's book *Your Battles Belong to the Lord.*

Print book interior design by Bart Dawson.

ISBN: 9781546015253

Printed in China

APS

10 9 8 7 6 5 4 3 2 1

Introduction

Women are a precious gift from God to the world. They are creative, sensitive, compassionate, intelligent, talented, and, according to the Bible, equal to men.

But many of us have lost the confidence God wants us to enjoy. Many of us have been left with vague feelings that we are somehow "less" than men. Less valuable. Less worthy. The end result is a society filled with insecure people, which can cause great difficulty in personal relationships.

God has a wonderful plan for your life and I pray that this journal will help you enter it more fully than ever before. It's my prayer that the quotes and encouragements in this journal will be an effective tool to help you gain the confidence God wants for you. You can hold your head up high and be filled with confidence about yourself and your future. Be bold and step out to do new things—even things no man or woman has ever done before. You have what it takes!

*W*omen need to experience a revival of knowing
their infinite worth and value.

[God's] desire is that you be bold, courageous, confident, respected, admired, promoted, sought after, and, most of all, loved.

Confident people do not concentrate on their weaknesses; they develop and maximize their strengths.

....

....

....

....

....

....

....

....

....

....

....

....

....

....

....

....

....

....

....

Confidence allows us to face life with boldness, openness, and honesty.
It enables us to live without worry and to feel safe.
It enables us to live authentically.

*When it comes to fulfilling promises,
God does not discriminate.*

....

....

....

....

....

....

....

....

....

....

....

....

....

....

....

....

....

When we have confidence in God and His love and kindness,
we can progress to living confidently and
enjoying the life He wants for us.

"*A*chieve" comes before "Believe" in the dictionary,
but the order is switched in real life.

*F*ear does not mean you are a coward. It only means that you need to be willing to feel the fear and do what you need to do anyway.

*Courage is not the absence of fear; it is action in the presence of fear.
Bold people do what they know they should do—
not what they feel like doing.*

When we know we are loved for ourselves
and not just our accomplishments or performance,
we no longer need to fear failure.

*I*t is much better to let God heal you than to spend your life being bitter about the past.

Jesus said there is no more male or female—we are all one in Him.
The total sum of our worth and value is based on who we are in Christ.

If a married couple can handle themselves the way God intended, their relationship will be wonderful and unbelievably fruitful.

$\mathcal{I}$t is time for you to have a healthy self-respect, balanced self-love, and a firm, unshakeable confidence in God and the gifts, talents, and abilities that He has placed inside of you.

If God did not want to use women in ministry, why did He include them in the most important events in Jesus' life?

---

*D*on't let anyone ever tell you that God cannot or will not use you,
just because you are a woman.

[A confident woman] does not fear being unloved, because she knows first and foremost that God loves her unconditionally.

Love is the healing balm that the world needs, and God offers it freely and continuously. His love is unconditional. He does not love us IF; He simply and for all time loves us.

To know that you are loved by someone you can trust is the best
and most comforting feeling in the world.

The Bible says in 1 John 4:18 that the perfect love of God casts out fear. When fear does not rule us, we are free to be bold and confident.

*F*aith is confidence in God and a belief that His promises are true.

_____

_____

_____

_____

_____

_____

_____

_____

_____

_____

_____

_____

_____

_____

_____

_____

_____

_____

_____

_____

_____

_____

We cannot walk in the vanity of our own mind, in our feelings, and our own will and ever experience victory in our lives. God says, "Fear not," and we must be determined that we will obey Him in this area.

*F*ear is the darkroom where all of your negatives are developed, so why not look at the brighter side of life?

God is positive, and that is His reality. It is the way He is, the way He thinks, and the way He encourages us to be.

A person is not a failure because she tried some things that did not work out. She fails only when she stops trying.

Thinking negatively prevents you from being aggressive, bold, and confident. Why not think positively and walk with confidence?

I believe confidence is found in doing the best we can with what we have to work with and not in comparing ourselves with others and competing with them.

*P*salm 139 teaches us that God intricately formed each of us
in our mothers' wombs with His own hand and that He wrote
all of our days in His book before any of them took shape.

*Appreciate others for what they are and enjoy
the wonderful person you are.*

*C*elebrate your uniqueness and rejoice in the future
God has planned for you.

We can benefit from our strengths and overcome our weaknesses through [God's] help.

*G*od works through our faith, not our fear.

If God is asking you to step out into something that is uncomfortable for you, I can assure you that when you take the step of faith, you will find Him walking right beside you.

....
....
....
....
....
....
....
....
....
....
....
....
....
....
....
....
....
....
....

Have a positive, aggressive, take-action attitude, and you
will enjoy your life more. It may be difficult at first,
but it will be worth it in the end.

*M*ake a decision that with God's help you will be the person He intended you to be and you will have the life He wants you to have.

*I*f we will just give God what we have, He will use it
and give us back more than we had to begin with.

The Bible says that God created everything we see out of "things that are unseen," so I have decided that if He can do that, surely He can do something with my little bit—no matter how unimpressive it is.

*I*t is not our abilities that God desires,
but it is our availability He wants.

If you pay more attention to your thoughts and choose to think on things that will help you instead of hinder you, it will release God's power to help you be the confident woman God wants you to be.

A spiritually mature woman will be the first to do what is right even if nobody else is doing so.

Making the effort to do things with excellence always makes me feel better about myself and increases my confidence.

....

....

....

....

....

....

....

....

....

....

....

....

....

....

....

....

....

....

....

....

....

....

....

....

Have a plan and work your plan. Be disciplined to your plan unless God shows you something else He wants you to do.

If we do what we can do, God will always do what we cannot do.

I encourage you not to look merely at your work but look also at the promise of reward. Take time to enjoy the fruit of your labor and you'll be energized to finish your course.

We are not created by God to waste anything he has given us, and time is certainly one of the greatest assets we have.

*P*ut a smile on someone else's face, and your own joy will increase.

You don't have to be guilty and condemned; you can admit your sins, and ask God to forgive you, and to cleanse you in the blood of Jesus.

*K*nowing you are prepared for whatever comes will increase
your confidence in an amazing way.

We can speak words that build confidence in ourselves and others or we can speak words that destroy confidence.

[*A* confident woman] can recover from making a mistake and doesn't allow the fear of making one to imprison her or tie her up in self-doubt.

We need to believe God's Word more than we believe our feelings.

If our hearts are sincere and we are honestly seeking God's will, even if we do make a mistake, He will intervene and get us back on track.

Doubt is a fear of negative things happening, but faith expects good things to take place.

*O*nce a person's willpower is renewed by God's Word and they know enough to choose good over evil, they become very dangerous to Satan and his kingdom of darkness.

You can train yourself to be positive in what appears to be a negative situation.

You will be amazed at the exciting things that happen to you
if you speak God's Word instead of how you feel.

Study God's Word and you will find out that you are precious, created in your mother's womb by God's own hand. You are not an accident.

*B*elieve that you make good decisions, that you are a valuable person with a great future and something good is going to happen to you today.

Trust doesn't just appear in our lives, but it grows as we take steps of faith and experience God's faithfulness.

*G*od will use everything in your life to train you if you are
willing to be trained.

We are nothing without [Christ] and yet we can do everything with Him.

....

....

....

....

....

....

....

....

....

....

....

....

....

....

....

....

....

....

God is looking for people with experience in life so ask Him
to begin your training and preparation today and you can learn
anything you will need for your future.

Don't despise the days of small beginnings.
Those small beginnings are usually all we can handle at the time.
God will give more when He knows we are ready.

*Y*our faith-filled actions are seeds you sow. Sow your seed in faith, and God will bring a harvest at just the right time.

Insecurity and a lack of confidence will steal the wonderful life that God has planned for you.

*M*ake positive affirmations to yourself every day about your qualities.
Jesus came to take care of what you could not do
so let Him do His job and thank Him for it.

I have been walking with God most of my life and I am still learning the importance of not trying to do anything without praying.

....

....

....

....

....

....

....

....

....

....

....

....

....

....

....

....

....

....

....

....

*Prayer opens the door for God to work in our lives, situations,
and the lives of our loved ones.*

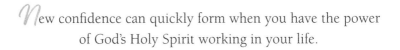

*N*ew confidence can quickly form when you have the power
of God's Holy Spirit working in your life.

The devil may be against you, but God is for you; and with Him
on your side you absolutely cannot lose.

God uses men and women who are set on obeying and pleasing Him, not those who are controlled by the fear of man.

*M*any people who have done great things in life were willing
to stand alone and that is not possible without confidence.

*C*elebrate the fact that you're not exactly like everyone else.
You are special! You are unique!

*O*ur worth is not found in being different or the same as others;
it is found in God.

God will always strengthen those who are willing to look their weaknesses in the face and say, "You cannot stop me."

....

....

....

....

....

....

....

....

....

....

....

....

....

....

....

....

....

....

....

When fear comes knocking on your door, let faith answer.

*W*e cannot do anything properly without [God] and should be dependent on God at all times for all things.

*N*eeding God and needing people is not a sign of weakness.
We can be dependent and independent at the same time.

It has been statistically proven that 10% of people will never like you, so stop trying to have a perfect record with everyone and start celebrating who you are.

When an unhappy person is unsuccessful in making you unhappy
they begin to respect and admire you.

I finally decided that if God is happy with me, that is enough.

We are not created by God to merely do the same thing over and over until it has no meaning left at all. God is creative... He is full of surprises and yet totally dependable.

*W*isdom knows when to keep quiet and when to talk.

I believe that not being true to one's own self is
one of the biggest joy thieves that exists.

*A*lways remember that to establish independence
you must not be a pretender. Be yourself!

*F*ollow your heart and keep your peace.
Say "no" when you need to and "yes" when you should.

God created us to be individuals who are able to work together
for the common good of all.

I look for people to be a blessing to because I have learned the vitally important lesson that Jesus taught about walking in love.

*Don't just put in your time here on earth; enjoy your life
and make the world glad that you are here.*

*G*od is all you have. Many other things are nice and comforting,
but God is the only person we can never do without.

$\mathcal{M}$y confidence must be in [God] more than it is in anything or anyone else.

If we ever want to overcome uncertainty and doubt, if we ever truly want to become confident women, it's vital that we have a complete and thorough understanding of the nature and anatomy of fear.

Anything hidden has power over us, but once it is brought into the light it can be dealt with and overcome.

_____

_____

_____

_____

_____

_____

_____

_____

_____

_____

_____

_____

_____

_____

_____

_____

_____

As we learn to use prayer to confront and combat the small fears,
[God] will help us learn to tackle bigger fears too.

*W*hen we do our part, praying and stretching our spiritual muscles as we take these steps of faith, God always does His part, making seemingly impossible things possible.

....
....
....
....
....
....
....
....
....
....
....
....
....
....
....
....
....
....
....
....
....
....

God's promises are not for a specially selected few people;
they are for everyone.

*R*eplace your fears with confidence and watch what God can do!

*G*od never intended us to run from our enemies.
His plan was and still is that with Him at our side we confront
any issue in our life that is a problem.

[God] tells us to stand firm with a belt of truth, a breastplate of righteousness, shoes of the gospel of peace, a shield of faith, a helmet of salvation, and the sword of the Spirit.

The way to develop confidence is to do the thing you fear, and get a record of successful experiences behind you.

*F*ace your fears today and ask God for His help in moving past them.
It is only by His grace that we can all overcome our fears!

Prayer opens the door for God to get involved
and meet our needs.

[God] has the future all planned and He knows the answer to everything. His Word promises us that He will take care of us if we trust in Him.

....

....

....

....

....

....

....

....

....

....

....

....

....

....

....

....

....

....

Confidence is the fruit of trusting God.

God's power is not available just to make unpleasant things in our lives go away; it is frequently available to walk us through them courageously.

_D_read is expecting something unpleasant to happen and it has nothing to do with faith. Faith looks forward to something good.

*C*onfidence in God is absolutely wonderful because it gives you the confidence that God has answers even when you don't.

*I*nstead of thinking that you cannot do things if you are afraid, make up your mind that you will do whatever you need to do even if you have to do it afraid.

*When we lean into the dilemma and trust the hand of God—
we gain control.*

....
....
....
....
....
....
....
....
....
....
....
....
....
....
....
....
....

Trust God that whatever your future holds He will enable you
to handle it when the time comes.

Too many people are not living their dreams because
they are living their fears.

Take some bold steps of faith and change anything
the Lord leads you to change.

When I think of what boldness looks like on someone,
I think of someone who is daring, courageous, brave, and fearless.

Genuinely brave people not only have the courage to take action, they also have the courage to wait when they need to.

Take each compliment that you receive as a rose, and at the end of the day take the entire bouquet and offer it back to God, knowing that it came from Him.

We don't need to know what God is going to do,
how He is going to do it, or when He is going to do it.
We only need to know that He is with us.

If we stare at our problems too much, think and talk
about them too much, they are likely to defeat us.
Glance at your problems but stare at Jesus.

....

....

....

....

....

....

....

....

....

....

....

....

....

....

....

....

....

....

Winning requires preparation, training, sacrifice, and a willingness to press past our opposition. It often requires falling many times and continuing to get up over and over again.

Cowards quit, but confidence and courage finish.

*C*onfidence is faith in God and a belief that because He is helping you,
you can succeed in whatever you need to do.

When trials and tribulations come, Satan will offer fear but God offers faith, courage, and confidence. Which one are you receiving?

....
....
....
....
....
....
....
....
....
....
....
....
....
....
....
....
....
....
....

*I*f a farmer plants tomato seeds, he will get a harvest of tomatoes.
If we plant encouragement in the lives of other people,
we will reap a harvest of encouragement in our own.

*A great woman doesn't allow fear to be her master.
She courageously looks it in the face and faces it down
with God by her side.*

*I*f you are the only one you know who is willing to do what is right,
then you be the one who will make a difference.

*D*on't just selfishly and fearfully pass through this life,
but do everything you can, every way you can,
for everyone that you can, as often as you can.

$\mathcal{E}$njoy the fact that God knew what He was doing and rely on the thought that surely God said the same thing about you as He did when He called the world into creation: "And it was good."

*If you wear a smile you will have friends,
if you wear a frown all you will have is wrinkles.*

*D*on't talk about yourself according to the way you feel or look.
Speak God's Word over your life.

If we really understood the power that is in words,
I think we would change the way we talk.

We cannot ask fearfully and expect to receive.
We must come to God's throne boldly.

*G*od is able to do exceedingly, abundantly, above and beyond
all that we could ever dare to hope, ask, or think.
Are you daring in prayer? Are you expecting enough?

BE confident even when you don't FEEL confident
and watch God work!

The door is wide open for you to realize your dreams.
Walk confidently into your future and never look back!

The life God has provided for us through Jesus Christ is a precious gift
and we should enjoy every moment of it.

*I*nstead of being afraid of something you are not familiar with, familiarize yourself with it. Do some research or ask some questions.

God's word teaches us that He has provided a good plan for
each person, yet they will never experience it unless they
know about it and also know how to access it.

Remember not to run from your fears; lean into them and you will conquer them.

*W*herever you are going, God has already been there
and paved the way for you.

You will be amazed at how much time you may have if you have a spirit-led schedule rather than a people-driven one.

....

....

....

....

....

....

....

....

....

....

....

....

....

....

....

....

....

A confident person can do more with less stress because they live with an ease that fearful people never experience.

Your priority is not to keep everyone else in your life happy by doing all the things they expect; it is to live a life that is pleasing to God and one that you can enjoy.

Just remember that God loves you and wants to use you
in powerful ways to help other people.

We cannot love ourselves unless we realize how much God loves us, and if we don't love ourselves, we cannot love other people.

*O*ne of the great things about a relationship with God is that
He always provides new beginnings.
His Word says that His mercy is new every day.

[God] purposely makes all of us different, and different is not bad;
it is God showing his creative variety.

Don't spend your life thinking "if only" you had something else,
then you could do something worthwhile.
"If only" is a thief of what could be.

*C*onfidence, trust, and security bring peace and rest to our souls.

Taking time to enjoy the fruit of your labors is one of the main things
that will help you keep pressing on in difficult times.

In my opinion, givers are powerful people; they are happy and fulfilled.

$\mathcal{S}$peaking kindly to other people is a tremendous attribute
and one that certainly enhances a godly woman.

Charm, grace, and beauty can be deceptive because they are not lasting, but the woman who reverently and worshipfully fears the Lord shall be praised.

When Satan wars against my mind, I can open my mouth and say out loud what God's Word says about me, and you can do the same thing.

God once told me that if I didn't trust myself, then I didn't trust Him.
He said that He was living in me, and directing, guiding,
and controlling me because I asked Him to do so.
I needed to believe God's promises, not my feelings or thoughts.

*P*ractice trusting yourself rather than doubting yourself.

*B*elieve that God wants to meet your needs because He is good,
not necessarily because you are good. None of us living in
a fleshly body has a perfect record; we all make mistakes and yours
probably are no worse than anyone else's. So stop beating up on yourself
and start expecting God to be God in your life.